HOW BRITAIN WON THE SPACE RACE

The British Space Ship Under Construction
This photograph (courtesy Tass) gives a splendid idea of the 'geophrenic' method of warptrussing the outer pressure hull. The natural flora were later removed by Order of the Select Committee.

HOW BRITAIN WON THE SPACE RACE

by
Desmond Leslie
Fellow of the Royal Astronautical Society
Emeritus Professor of Ufology (Oxon, Cantab)
Reader in Osculations (U.C.L.A., T.C.D., U.C.H.)
and
Patrick Moore
Founder President of the Schrimpwisl Society
Reader in Lunacy (Greenwich)
Honorary Volcano Controller to the Mexican Government

Mitchell Beazley London

CONTENTS

Mitchell Beazley Limited
Artist's House, 14-15 Manette Street,
London W1

First published 1972

Cover and colour illustrations
by Alan Cracknell

Designed by Janette Palmer

Printed and bound in Great Britain
by Cox & Wyman, Fakenham

ISBN 0 85533 011 2

FOREWORD

Much has been heard of Russian, American, Chinese and even French achievements in space. Rockets have been despatched; endless small satellites clutter up the available orbits round our planet, carrying out every conceivable programme in every possible direction. The names of von Braun, Goddard, Lovell and others are known to all. Yet how many people have heard, even know, of Schrimpwisl, Dreikleinen, von Drein and ffryde-Fischer?

It has generally been thought that Great Britain, due to Government apathy and overspending on futile projects, has been left sadly behind in the field of astronautics. It has even been said that our sole ambition, in the future, is to hire a rocket or two from America and eventually put up a communications satellite of our own, so that the Post Office can continue with its policy of increasing charges and deteriorating service.

This is not the case. What has not so far been revealed to the general public is that a British pressure group of space scientists was at work long before Sputnik I climbed into the sky. Led by ffryde-Fischer and other patriotic Britons (including Schrimpwisl, von Drein and Dreikleinen) they had determined to see that the Union Jack should fly over the Moon (despite the lack of air) before the Hammer and Sickle or the Stars and Stripes could do so.

Their means were limited. So, for that matter, were their brains. But their hearts were true, and their resolution unshakable. Naturally, they had to make do and improvise, preferring to use existing traditional materials rather than waste time and money on needless research.

This may explain why some of the Top Secret materials shown here bear a superficial resemblance to those used in the Great Exhibition of 1851, and may appear slightly familiar to the Editors of the *Illustrated London News*, among other scientific journals.

But the end result was triumph – though so far an unpublicised one. Britain has not only reached the Moon, but won the most important space race of all: that of interstellar travel. And so it is with humility, and pride, that we tell the full story. The names of the British team will long resound through the furthest confines of Whitehall, the City of Westminster, Outer Space, and Bovey Tracey.

Patrick Moore

THE CHARACTER

Herr Doktor Silenus Schrimpwisl

Sir Humphrey ffryde-Fischer Bt O.M.

OF THIS HISTORY

Dr. Gottfried von Doppelganger

THE SELECT COMMITTEE

These five portraits depict the real pioneers of space research. Unfortunately most of them cannot be named, or even recognized. The Select Committee was dissolved in 1955, following the repeal of Avogadro's Law.

SIR HUMPHREY'S BLUEPRINTS
EXTRAVEHICULAR VISORS.
HELMET
(THERMALLY CONTROLLED)
VHF
ANTENNA LINK
To SPACE CRAF
PEN LIGHT POCKET
LUNAR MODULE
RESTRAINT RING
NOSE
CONE
COCOA
FLUNGE VA
TREMULAT
LUNAR OVERSHOES
Things to take.
Shaving kit.
Snuff.
Change of underclothing

SIR HUMPHREY'S TEAM ON THE LUNAR SURFACE

RETURN OF THE EXPEDITION
ERIN

PIONEER ATTEMPTS

The Ur-Apollo *above*
An early conception of space flight attributed to Von Rheingold. (Impractical).

In the following pages is unfolded the true story of how Sir Humphrey ffryde-Fischer triumphantly captained the British expedition to the Moon; of the brilliant individualist, Dr Silenus Schrimpwisl, and his limitless courage in the face of failure; and of his adversary in international scientific debate, Gottfried von Doppelganger. But before triumph comes the trial, and first we must look back.

Obviously, the idea of space flight is not new. It was not Greek in origin, as is often claimed. The first scientific suggestion was made by a Briton, Kurd von Rheingold. However, his design – given here – was never actually tested. Von Rheingold eventually emigrated to Australia.

Early Trials *right*
An interesting (and rare) photo of Sir Humphrey ffryde-Fischer Bt. embarking his crew for a trial flight in the helicopter which he designed specially for use in the higher turbulent atmosphere of Venus.

Sir Humphrey's Belief *right*
Sir Humphrey ffryde-Fischer attempting to change Boyle's Law.

Early in his career ffryde-Fischer became convinced that something was seriously wrong with the theoretic analysis of space flight. He came to the conclusion that the root of the trouble was Boyle's Law, and he set out to disprove it, or at least to change it.

In those first days, much theoretical work was carried out by Sir Humphrey. His researches were particularly meritorious in view of the fact that they naturally had to be undertaken out of the cricket season. From a practical viewpoint his rocket launching

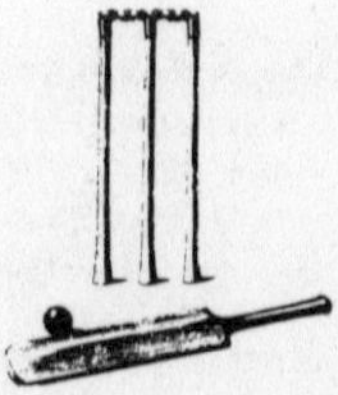

The Good Old Days *below*
Early attempt by ffryde-Fischer to fire projectiles to the Moon from Kingston Bagpuize, for which he was rusticated from Oxford.

The Anti-Gravity Experiment ***below***
An important experiment which was a strong influence in Schrimpwisl's subsequent calculations. Arrowed is Hochliebstraume, who offered to assist Sophomore Eva Washenbokker with her researches. Using the Moonwalk Simulator, Hochliebstraume achieved a record 'Time into EVA' of 10 hrs. 53 mins. They are now happily married.

attempt from Kingston Bagpuize marked the beginning of an era. One space probe is thought to have reached orbit and to have made planetfall with a small asteroid; this was confirmed by astronomers at Palomar Observatory, who detected the shock waves. Unfortunately nothing further was heard from the probe, and it was officially held that Sir Humphrey's plan of the universe contained some notable deviations.

In early 1950 an interesting and well attended demonstration in Anti-Gravity (Levitation) was given

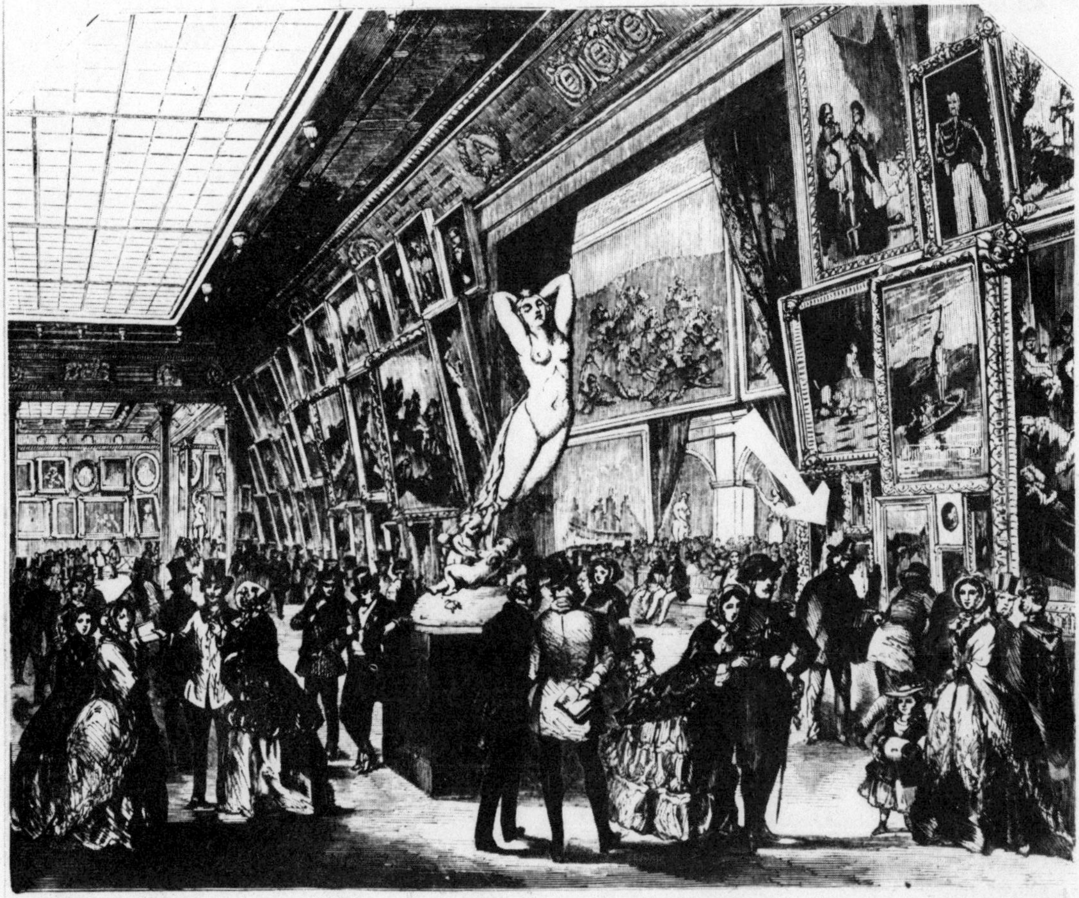

in the Founders' Hall at Cal Tech, California, U.S.A., by Sophomore Eva Lee Washenbokker. Only Hochliebstraume (arrowed) immediately realised the possibilities and offered to assist Sophomore Washenbokker with her researches.

At about the same time, Professor E. R. I.

Niggleton delivered his famous lecture to the Aetherius Society at Battersea Polytechnic. It was here that he made his celebrated pronouncement that $i(d-4) = 0$. Obviously, this altered the entire conception of space research dynamics, and explained why the levitation (anti-gravity) experiments at Cal Tech so signally failed to work. Much of Niggleton's subsequent career is shrouded in mystery. His most recent publication is *The Dating of Prehistoric Oriental Figurines* (The Laxative Press, Potter's Bar, 1967).

It was after Niggleton's revelations, and the levitation failure, that Schrimpwisl began energetic practical research. From his laboratory on Selsey Bill he threw himself whole-heartedly into his work. On one occasion he also threw himself into the sea, together with the shattered parts of his pioneer rocket, code named NUTS (Nuclear Unguided Test Ship). Now, too, began the Controversy with Doppelganger which lasted for so many years, and seems destined to continue indefinitely.

Niggleton's Lecture ***above***
Prof. E. R. I. Niggleton lecturing to the Aetherius Society at Battersea Polytechnic, with the aid of model flying saucers (Martian) seen on the shelf above him.

THE CONTROVERSY BEGINS

Schrimpwisl reading his Paper *above*
The memorable meeting of the Royal Astronautical Society at Burlington House on the night of June 4th 1950.

In the picture can clearly be seen the massed audience at Burlington House on that memorable night of June 4th 1950, a few moments before the start of the Controversy, and Schrimpwisl's expulsion from the Royal Astronautical Society. Schrimpwisl arose, and began eloquently to propose his theories, and his intention of proving them. But before long the adherents of Gottfried von Doppelganger grew noisy.

The root of the problem was that Doppelganger realised with Einstein that a body moving faster than light would travel backwards through time, and con-

Schrimpwisl's First Attempt *right*
About which very little is known, particularly by the Professor Doktor himself.

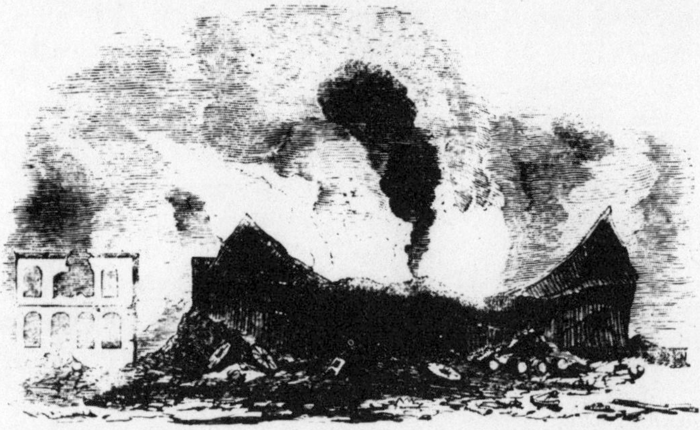

cluded correctly that a body travelling faster than time would conversely travel backwards through light.

Expressing these two functions graphically as curves, he was nonplussed to discover that even if extended indefinitely, they would never quite meet. The point where they nearly met (but didn't quite) was called 'The Discrepancy'; later 'Doppelganger's Discrepancy', and is expressed by the formulae:

$$\frac{L}{20} = s \text{ when } \frac{s}{12} = d \text{ whereas } \frac{L}{100} = p \text{ when } L \text{ is } 0.$$

If this were not so, space flight would be impossible.

Schrimpwisl's Second Attempt *left*
Owing to the purely academical error on the part of his staff, the nose of the rocket had been pointed towards the Earth instead of the more customary 'Away from Earth' position. Otherwise the attempt was completely successful.

Dreikleinen's Flying Saucer ***above***
Dreikleinen demonstrating his $\frac{1}{2}$-scale working model flying saucer before a select and sceptical gathering at Mount Palomar Observatory, Palomar Mountain, California, U.S.A.

Meanwhile, quite independently of Schrimpwisl and his team another British worker, Heinrich Dreikleinen, was experimenting with a disk shaped space craft. At one stage he transferred it to the United States, but met with a cool reception and returned in dudgeon to the friendly shores of Great Britain. Following an abortive attempt to land in the grounds of the Royal Observatory, Herstmonceux Castle, he brought his

Dreikleinen at Herstmonceux *above* Dreikleinen encountering stiff opposition from the Astronomer Royal and his staff.

craft down safely in the Serpentine. Since, however, it was unable to fly at any altitude greater than thirty feet, its use as a lunar vehicle was questionable.

Using a more successful full sized model, Dreikleinen again attempted to land his flying saucer at the Royal Observatory. This attempt was foiled only by diligent counter action of the Astronomer Royal and his staff, who have a long-standing aversion to flying saucers.

Hardware Development

Rocket Engines on the Test Bed
right
(Courtesy of the Royal Aircraft Establishment, Farnborough)
The palm trees, elephants and other apparatus were employed to produce realistic tropical conditions.

On the opposite page is a Top Secret photograph of ARMAGEDDON, the Automatic, Radionic, Magnetic and Gravitational Electronic (Doppelganger Discrepancy) Omniversal Numerator, to give its full name to the colossal calculator covering thirteen acres at Runnymede. The machine was in continuous operation for eight weeks to make the calculations necessary for reaching the Moon.

The laboratory assistant (arrowed) had been using it at the time this picture was taken to determine once and for all whether or not the very hairs of her head were numbered.

ARMAGEDDON held out great promise, but at the

ARMAGEDDON *below*
The largest electronic computer in the free world and a triumph of British electronic genius.

Take-off Ramps at Woomera *above*
Greasing the long take-off ramps at Woomera, Australia, in preparation for Schrimpwisl's third attempt to reach the Moon.

crucial moment it faltered. It had been asked to calculate the precise trajectory for a chemically fuelled probe to be launched to the Moon at escape velocity, and with an orbital inclination of 24° 32′. Unfortunately all it did was to produce, in the compartment marked 'Answer', a small lemon. Schrimpwisl attributed this failure to mice in the gunge-wheels.

The launching of the first Russian and American artificial satellites came as a considerable surprise to Schrimpwisl, who had been conducting futile experiments with exotic chemical fuels such as obscine. Alcohol had been tried, following publication of the American plans, but had been abandoned simply because the entire supply was consumed by the staff of the rocket base on Walpurgis Night. Little need be said about the third and fourth attempts, both carried out from Australia. Schrimpwisl had omitted to bear in mind that since Australia is at the bottom of the Earth, any launching from there will send a rocket down instead of up. When reminded of this, he uttered

Disaster Narrowly Averted *above*
The end of Schrimpwisl's third attempt.

the old fashioned Anglo-Saxon oath 'Blitzen!' and returned to Selsey Bill. Much of the equipment was jettisoned; some was removed by watching Soviet agents to the USSR Kosmodrom, and the unused rocket propellant was bought by the Woollongabba Rotary Club to be used as manure on garden allotments.

Above is a Reuter photograph of the Number One section of the Three-Stage Rocket which was prematurely jettisoned over the Pacific Ocean, instead of in the English Channel as envisaged. One possible explanation could be that the Professor was in the central reaction chamber at the time of lift-off to see if it was firing correctly, with the result that only the right-hand bank of rocket motors fired. Schrimpwisl was found to be suffering from mild seasickness. Apart from that he declined to make a statement.

By 1963 the situation for the British team had become critical. Schrimpwisl's limited budget (17s. 6d. p.a.) was probably responsible for the failure of his fifth

Schrimpwisl's Fourth Attempt *below*
About which, the least said, the better.

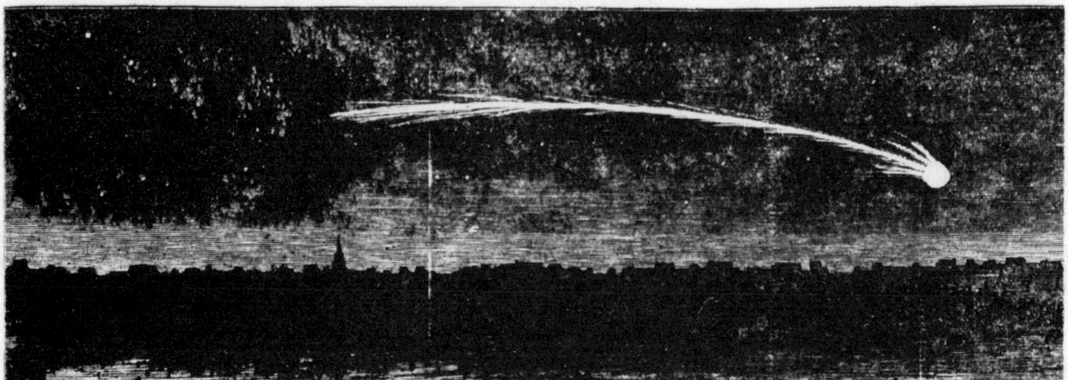

Schrimpwisl's Fifth Attempt ***above***
Schrimpwisl's rocket as it plunged into the sea at Lyme Regis on January 1st 1963. Interested spectators had climbed on to the wreck of the *Hesperus* in order to obtain a better view.

attempt. Lack of finance meant that little design progress was made. Nevertheless, Lundy was chosen as the new launching site, being nearer the English Channel, and a new trajectory was calculated. However, from a comparison of the photograph above with that of Schrimpwisl's Fourth Attempt, on the previous page, it is obvious that the flight paths, and the mistakes, were exactly the same. The rocket was subsequently recovered, but was of no further use for space travel, and the dismantled hull was made into lobster pots. However, for ffryde-Fischer and his colleagues brighter times were ahead. Once Doppelganger had discovered his Discrepancy the path to the Moon was opened. In 1963 the Discrepancy was twenty-five years old, and ffryde-Fischer and his colleagues were almost ready to set foot on that path. The proposed Lunar Expedition Team were immensely encouraged when Mrs Chigwell's sister agreed to supervise tea during the journey, and Niggleton's new pamphlet, *The Parliamentary System in Minoan Crete*, provided a further incentive.

More importantly the repeatedly successful despatch of both Russian and American space vehicles initiated the famous rivalry of East versus West. The approach of both teams is typified by the respective designs of the adjustable take-off couches. The clean, functional lines of the one, and the grand, imperialistic, decorative manner of the other speak clearly for the philosophies of the men who created them.

But in this controversy, at least, the British team took no part. It is still uncertain whether Niggleton's work *Sludge Systems in Old Sumeria* has any conceivable connection with the space programme.

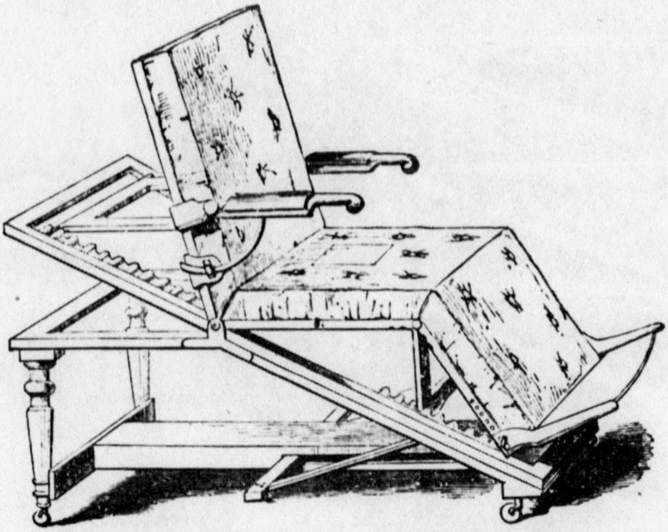

The National Couch *left*
Take-off couch in the American rocket.

The People's Couch *left*
Take-off couch in the Russian rocket, *Komsomol Kulturkollectivylych.*

Final Preparations

BOSS *above*
A sectional cut-away view of the British Orbital Space Station (BOSS).

In spite of the evidence of Russian and American developments, Sir Humphrey's researches finally came to fruition. With BOSS, the British Orbital Space Station, the Union Jack could at last flutter proudly in the field of astronautics. It was a technical triumph, and contained all modern essential refinements: an altimeter, a retro-rocket control, a bridge table, chess sets, newspaper racks for *The Times*, an automatic tea-making machine and much besides. As it made its first ascent into orbit, both the spectators burst into wild applause.

The picture above shows the ingenious interior arrangement. Perhaps the most novel feature is the huge relief map of the world covering the entire interior walls, by comparison with which the crew will be able to recognise instantly any part of the Earth's surface over which they may happen to be orbitting. Such innovation is typical of the British Genius displayed by Von Drein, Dreikleinen, Schrimpwisl and the other scientists who put Britain where she is in space today.

The second ascent, from the White City, was even more astonishing for its technological achievement.

BOSS is seen here being manoeuvred towards its launching ramp at the White City Stadium. At an exactly pre-determined moment, the great piece of space hardware slowly ascended the Ascent Ramp continuing on without mishap to descend the Descent Ramp on the other side, before an enthralled crowd of onlookers and experts.

The then Prime Minister, the Rt. Hon. Harold Wilson, had hoped to perform the launching ceremony, but was in fact unable to be present, since he had undertaken to assume the Chair at a meeting of the Anglo-Rhodesian Society. The ceremony was therefore carried out, in his stead, by the Secretary of the Woolwich Parish Council. The conversation between the astronauts inside BOSS was broadcast by the BBC, and Von Drein's typically English comment of 'Ach! zo!' is worthy to rank with Neil Armstrong's 'One Small Step'.

The Great Moment *below*
Launching BOSS, the British Orbital Space Station, named *Erin* after the initials of Professor (now Lord) E. R. I. Niggleton, its designer.

Main Control Room, BOSS ***above***
Here shown as it was being laid out under the direction of the President of the R.A.S., Sir Humphrey ffryde-Fischer Bt. O.M. etc. For security reasons, the Top Secret instruments were removed to the opposite page while this photograph was being taken.

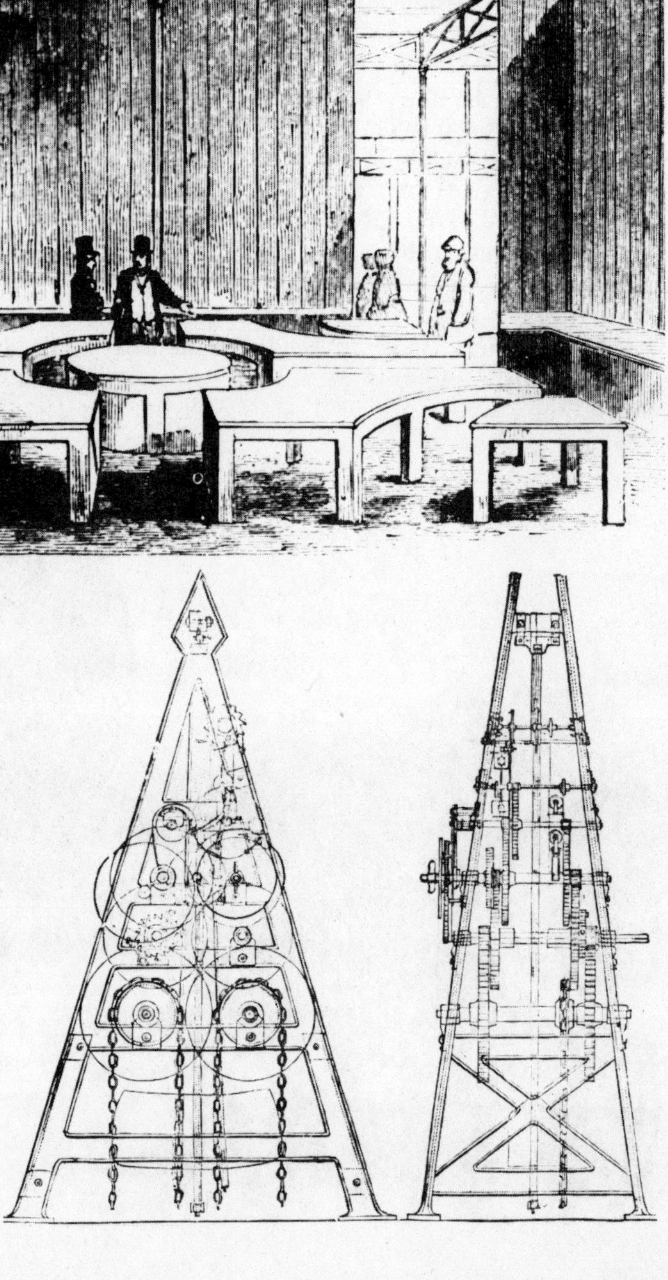

British Lunar Rocket ***right***
Section through the nose cone
1. Seen E. to W.
2. Seen S. to N.
The outer covering was replaced before blast-off.

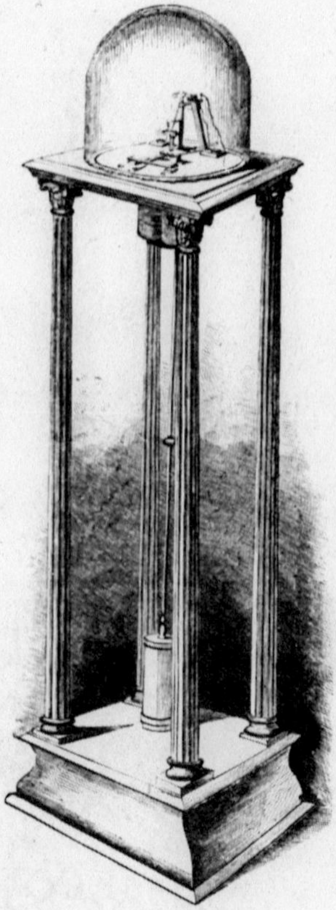

The Top Secret Instruments
These were removed from the Control Room on the opposite page for reasons of security.

above: Three Dimensional Televiewer (corrected for Doppelganger Discrepancy and Paraphase).

top left: Lunar clock for telling the time on the day side of the Moon only.

left: Flunge-valve tremulator, combining negative and calysthenical reactions in pralaya; also adaptable for mixing cocoa in weightless (zero g) conditions.

During the experiments, various new navigational aids were introduced. Care was also taken to make the interior of the space ship as comfortable as possible.

Hopworth's pocket Astronavigator made great strides forward and became a standard item of equipment for each astronaut, along with his notebook, pencil, whistle, chocolate, and regulation length of string.

Meanwhile Schrimpwisl pursued his own course.

Interim Experiment *above*
The combined forces of Schrimpwisl and Uprichard were no more successful than Schrimpwisl's efforts alone.

For some years he concentrated on theoretic research, perusing, pondering on, and puzzling over his adversary's Discrepancy. But Schrimpwisl was a determined man, and eventually began practical tests once more. For a time he joined forces with Uprichard and the photograph here shows the scene during their intermediate and quite pointless attempt (egged on by Von Drein) on May 13th, 1968.

Frau Doktor Schrimpwisl, the Professor's wife, mounted a pedestal (top right) with her two assistants from May 13th to May 19th, until the Doktor decided to come down again.

With the Moon now within the reach of British astronauts, attention was given to the design of a Lunar Roving Vehicle. This was originally proposed by Uprichard, whose patent was in many ways superior to that subsequently used by the astronauts of Apollos 15, 16 and 17. The chassis was mounted on exterior whimples, and the lidgeons were floated in a

solution of oxo; a revolutionary innovation was the provision of extra grunges to prevent pitch and yaw. The vehicle was tested on the main road outside Birmingham, but the driver lost his way in the complicated roundabouts, and the Moon car has never been seen since.

Uprichard's Lunar Tractor *above*
The design was rejected.

THE TRIUMPH

The Moon Landing ***above***
Instant construction activity followed the triumphant moonfall of BOSS.

The Moon at last! On July 20th 1969 at 1623 hrs (G.M.T.) BOSS made safe moonfall in a small, rather chilly, craterlet within the mighty crater Plato, which was selected for its simple logic.

There were, inevitably, some delays. When BOSS was put into lunar orbit, ffryde-Fischer, von Drein and their colleagues regarded it as prudent to make a test of the lunar atmosphere, in case it proved to be toxic. They had equipped themselves with sensitive recording instruments, but as the Moon has no atmosphere they spent three weeks in abortive theorizing while all the instruments registered zero. Eventually they took the plunge, and it is true to say that their landing was both fascinating and spectacular. At the time the precise details could not be revealed, for security reasons, which is why no announcement has been made until now.

The outer hull of BOSS was rapidly dismantled, its warp-trusses being 'caninalised' to form part of the pressure dome of the permanent lunar base. Working in full earthlight Sir Humphrey and his highly trained team soon had the main girders of the pressure dome in position. The work proceeded with amazing rapidity owing to the fact that lunar gravity is only one sixth of that experienced on Earth.

In the picture opposite, the small booth (right) was erected for the convenience of the erection team. The fake landscape, suggesting prior habitation, was superimposed optically as a later precaution against foreign press men.

The Priorities *above*
Magnificent Losby-Uprichard tea boilers ready for service.

Before long a Lunar Base was in full operation, and by the end of the first lunar day (equivalent to fourteen Earth-days) Sir Humphrey had completed the erection of the air locks, hydroponic nutrient system, radio transmitting installation, billiard table and practice cricket net.

As can be seen here, the four specially designed Losby-Uprichard Tea Boilers are already installed and ready for continuous service, only four hours after making moonfall. To the left of the picture exterior decorators are painting the attractive facade, with its

curtained doorway, of the quarters designed to house the Losby-Uprichard Tea Ladies, specially selected for their stability under low gravity conditions.

Meanwhile, back on Earth, the indomitable Schrimpwisl tried again, this time from a barge moored in the Thames Estuary off Gravesend. The attempt was no more, and no less, successful than any previous effort. Despite which, the Professor stubbornly still refuses to take any account of Doppelganger's Discrepancy. This, indeed, is the fine independent spirit of thought that has made our island unique.

Schrimpwisl's Seventh Attempt
above
The suspicious vessel in the background has recently been identified as an American sail training ship.

The scene before the British Pressurized Lunar Base, once it was complete, was extraordinarily touching. To a man, the loyal team under Sir Humphrey filed out to admire its simple functional design. Some got over excited and forgot to put on their space suits. Others were just showing off. All rapidly regretted their error.

But even at this stage scientific experiments were well under way. It was soon discovered, by tossing prepared blades of grass in an upward direction, that

there was little or no breeze on the Moon. To mitigate the heat of the full glare of the Lunar noon Sir Humphrey had stout poles erected (seen here on either side of the Pressure Dome) attached to which were the components of his patented Freeflow (Localised Air) Generating System.

It is unfortunate that Schrimpwisl himself was not with this first pioneer expedition. His seventh attempt did at least attract some publicity, and was the subject of a strong article on the back page of the *Gravesend Herald*.

Architecture of the Space Age
below
A magnificent view of the British Pressurised Lunar Base (BIPED) shortly after its completion in the Crater Plato.

The British Prototype *right*
BIPED, upon which design the colonies of space are quite likely to be based.

Above is an internal view of the spacious BIPED inflated to normal working pressure. Note the water purifying plant (left foreground) and the traditional (if unusual) design of the British space helmet. The large Bioflora (centre rear) produced an adequate supply of oxygen during the daylight hours. During the lunar night it was moved outside and covered up with cellophane. To the far right are detailed illustrations of the prototype fresh water purifying plant, seen before and after testing. Niggleton's most broadly based work, *Chlorophyll, Zulus and the United Nations* stems largely from the results of these tests.

Water Purifying Plant *above*
Before and after testing.

An Inferior Design *left*
The rather poor imitation of BIPED built by the Americans and now undergoing pressure tests at White Sands, New Mexico, where it sprang a leak.

A. Airlock
B. Observatory
C. Portholes
D. Television aerial and radar
E. Americans

Flora, Fauna, Sundry Artifacts

Seen Briefly in the Mare Imbrium
right
Sir Humphrey caught a glimpse of this remarkably well-preserved Fuel Induction System from a Pre-Dynastic solar boat similar to those used by Pharaoh Thothathmosis III, LCCXXXVL Dynasty. Dreikleinen, however, favours the theory that it was a sludge pump from the Lower Nile, abandoned in Imbrium by Leonardo da Vinci.

Lunar exploration proved to be immensely exciting. It is to be noted that Niggleton made a valuable contribution, even though ffryde-Fischer and others had completely forgotten that he had joined the expedition. On his return he published a further paper, *A Re-examination of the Manuscript of Bruckner's Seventh Symphony*, which will be included in the official report now being prepared.

During the preliminary surveys of the lunar surface, many interesting and unusual objects were discovered. First and foremost were the craters, which seemed to be in abundant supply and of natural origin.

But in the crater Gassendi, for example, a number of artifacts were uncovered by Niggleton which tended to suggest (though he is unwilling to comment firmly)

Found by Niggleton in Gassendi *left*
Carpet (by Aubusson) for use in flying saucer, or in small crater.

Gloyp *left*
Looking for augs. Unfortunately it bit the President instead.

previous expeditions to our satellite both by extinct terrestial races and by other life forms.

Life forms were, in fact, seen and photographed. The photograph of the Fuel Induction System (or sludge pump), for instance, was taken by Sir Humphrey very early one morning. In this he was extremely lucky since, startled by his footstep, the Pump (or system) moved rapidly away. But none of them, however, as far as can be ascertained, appear native to the planet.

A singular assortment of some of them are shown on these pages, prior to their eventual translation to the Astrophysical Section of the British Museum, now temporarily housed at Mrs Chigwell's Conservatories, Sunbury-on-Thames.

A Very Poor Show *above*
The British team gathered for a Martian's benefit.

In Crater Copernicus, the British Team were assembled, not without some modicum of inconvenience, in order to witness the purported hand-launching of a small flying saucer by a very large Martian.

As failure mounted upon failure, it became quite obvious, even to the layman, that the operator had never heard of Doppelganger's Discrepancy or, like Schrimpwisl, chose stonily to ignore it.

Desiring no further truck with the miserable fellow, Sir Humphrey led his disgusted team back to the comparative sanity of BIPED.

On August 14th 1969, three weeks after moonfall, Niggleton drew the President's attention to a quite large 'Venusian Type' flying saucer of conventional design and appearance which had, apparently, been abandoned outside the main entrance airlock of BIPED several centuries before the erection of the British Lunar Base.

The interior was in a truly sorry condition, the

crew, before leaving, having made little or no attempt to preserve its state of space worthiness. All attempts by Britain to make it saucershape were predoomed to failure, owing to asteroid rot.

Again the strict security precautions observed by Sir Humphrey and his team are shown in the re-touching of the photograph with a spurious background. But the lunar tractor, built to Uprichard's revised plans, is genuine, and visible to the left of the picture.

Lack of Public Spirit ***above***
The antique Venusian Saucer, found in a very sorry condition.

From these two disappointing experiences, the inference to be drawn is that it is impossible to count on finding much reliability or public spirit outside of Shakespeare's sceptred isle.

The Final Achievements

Perseverance Rewarded *above*
Before leaving Lunar Base and returning to Earth on August 21st 1969, Sir Humphrey made one final attempt to change Boyle's Law – and succeeded.

From the outset Sir Humphrey had been convinced that Boyle's Law was the key to certain enigmas which still remained in the realms of space exploration. The British expedition had achieved its undoubted success through careful consideration of Doppelganger's Discrepancy, Niggleton's pamphlets, Dreikleinen's saucer, and Mrs Chigwell's dog Wisden. But the question of Boyle's Law remained, and was only finally solved during Sir Humphrey's final Lunar Ramble. He raced back to BIPED, set up his instruments, and, as can be seen from the photograph, proved definitively his revolutionary theory.

Having thus succeeded in his main purpose, the President struck base and gave the orders for BOSS to be reassembled and readied for launching.

The return trip was completely uneventful, and the mighty British space craft made earth fall at Basingstoke on September 1st.

Sir Humphrey then set off, poste haste, to his country home at Bovey Tracey, where his family were joyously awaiting him.

Spurred on by news from the Moon, Schrimpwisl made one all out final attempt to equal the successes of his former associates and colleagues in the R.A.S.

and (prior to the inception of the Great Controversy) his very good friends.

Though not exactly pandering to Doppelganger, he did admit to certain theoretical postulates anent to his Discrepancy and, though not admitting their practical application did, in fact, concede to their partial relevance in a strictly limited (and strictly contained) sense.

The emotional effect of this partial (though by no means accepted) admission on his part may have caused him to overcorrect his compensations for

The Family at Home ***above***
Lady Ffryde Fischer and her two daughters on hearing of Sir Humphrey's safe return.

Schrimpwisl's Final Attempt *left*
Schrimpwisl's space rocket is seen here at zero minus 30, poised proudly on the launching pad. It was boosted by four midship rockets corrected, so he thought (but would not admit) for Discrepancy; and these are now believed to have been the main cause of overthrust, overboost and overshoot.

Until the final seconds of countdown, the rocket was besieged by anxious swarms of creditors and shareholders who feared, alas, that he would never return.

He didn't.

Meanwhile in London *above*
Consternation at the Royal Astronautical Society (Burlington House) on hearing of Schrimpwisl's successful arrival on Alpha Centauri.

The Last Word *right*
Schrimpwisl's triumphant message from Alpha Centauri being decoded at the Admiralty. The cleaning woman overlooking the First Lord's shoulder was later found to have been a Soviet spy.

Discrepancy Factor, which (if admitted) caused his vehicle to overshoot the Moon entirely, and proceed unhindered to Alpha Centauri where the Professor eventually made a safe landing by means of a wire mesh parachute filled with hydrogen.

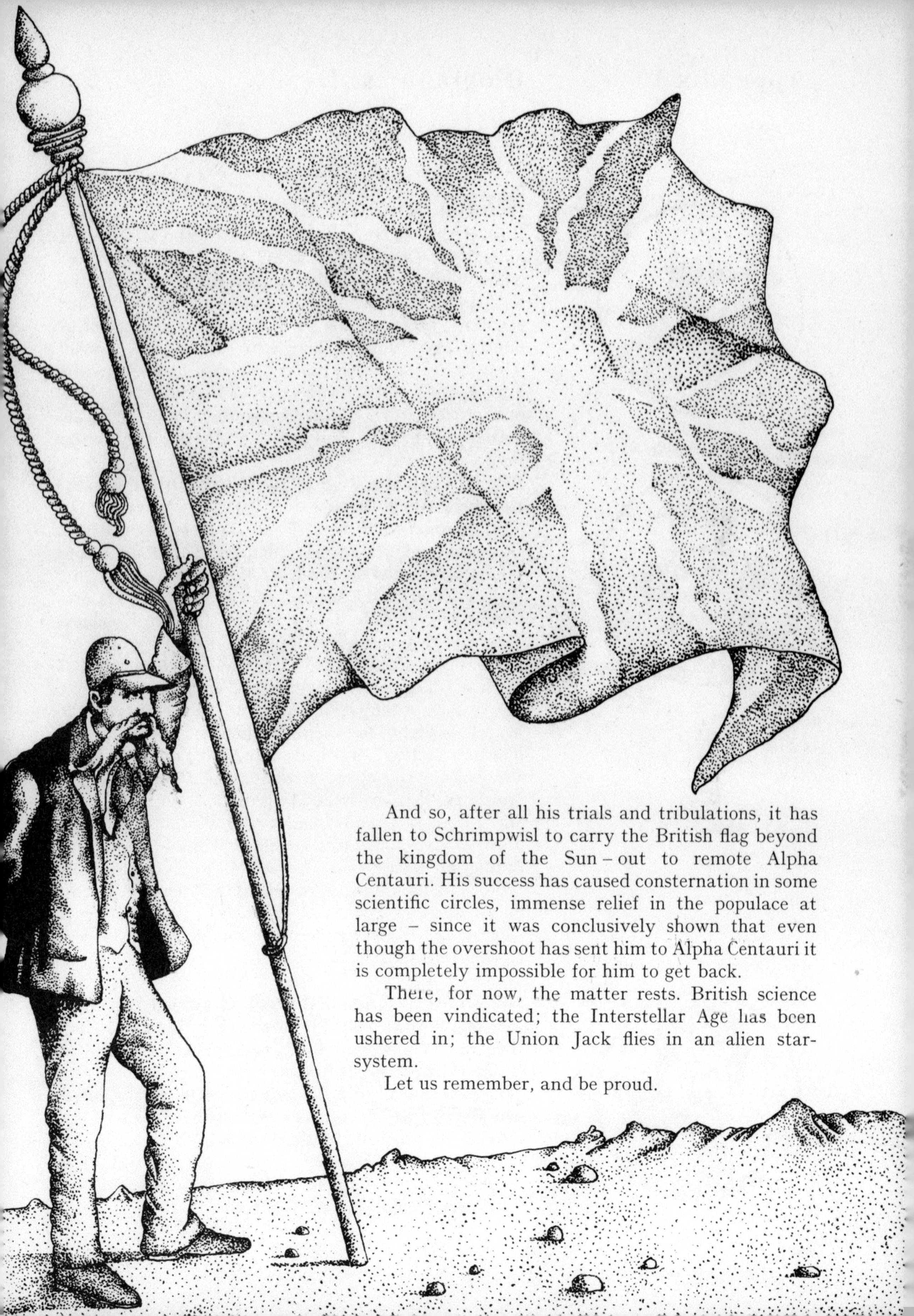

And so, after all his trials and tribulations, it has fallen to Schrimpwisl to carry the British flag beyond the kingdom of the Sun – out to remote Alpha Centauri. His success has caused consternation in some scientific circles, immense relief in the populace at large – since it was conclusively shown that even though the overshoot has sent him to Alpha Centauri it is completely impossible for him to get back.

There, for now, the matter rests. British science has been vindicated; the Interstellar Age has been ushered in; the Union Jack flies in an alien star-system.

Let us remember, and be proud.

Appendix I Biographical Details

SCHRIMPWISL, Dr. Silenus

Born Berne 1892. m. 1921 Dr. Prof. Berthilde, daughter of Margraf Odolf von und zu Alkaseltzichstein from whom he is now (probably permanently) separated by four and a half light years and with whom he had constant disagreements of a theoretical and scientific nature. A brilliant though unconventional rocket scientist whose revolutionary opinions have led him into sharp conflict with the orthodox school. His opinions led to 'The Great Controversy 1950–71' and to his expulsion from the R.A.S. (and the Solar System).

ffRYDE-FISCHER, Sir Humphrey Othur Marlemorency Chenonceaux de Chivvy Elderdendry OM

13th Baronet, only son of Sir Glanders Fischer 12th Baronet, and Muriel Upcrumpet of Fulham, born prematurely 1900 on the Loop the Loop at the White City Exhibition. Educated Eton, Harrow, Oxford, Cambridge; Squash Champion 1918. Captain Rounders Team, 1922. Colours Mah Jong and Shove Florin.

Became President Royal Astronautical Society 1935 when a calligraphical error in his father's will led to the Society being endowed with sufficient funds to install gaslight in their Burlington House Headquarters. Married 1931 Lady Pandora Malvolais-Coven-Warlock-Coven, eldest daughter of Earl of Melton Mowbray, and has issue: 1 Cassandra Muriel, b. 1939 and 2 Clarissa Circe Niobe Norah Lolita, b. 1941.

Successfully lobbied for the repeal of Boyle's Law 1969 during an expedition to the Moon, subscribed by private funds. Clubs: Athenaeum, Saddleroom, Brads, Senior Carlton, Travellers. Residence: Bachelor Appt. Albany W.1. Seat: ffischerwyck Manor, Bovey Tracey, Devon, England.

von DOPPELGANGER, Prof. Gottfried

One of the most eminent of the early pioneers. Born Breslau 1906. Engaged in rocket research while at Berlin High School, 1910. Left Berlin High School 1910. Joined Technical staff at Heidelberg University, 1918, and discovered his famous Discrepancy there, 1938. Psychiatric treatment having failed, he engaged in a sharp controversy with Schrimpwisl, 1950–71. For further details of his academic career, see Schrimpwisl, *Der Schweinhund* (Leipzig 1952).

Appendix II Chronological Summary

B.C. 500,000,000,000,000	First natural spaceships, *eg* suns, comets, planets, etc.
5,000,000	First known flying creatures (organic), *eg* archaeopteryx, pterodactyl, pterracotta, pteddibhoys, etc.
10,000 – 4,000	Descents by Olympians to Earth, return journeys delayed owing to political and emotional complications.
5,000	First solar boats, built by Egyptian Pharaohs, described by Herodotus, considered apocryphal by Glumbucket.
2,000	Icarus – Schrimpwisl's ancestor.
1,000	Mars Persona of Clusium.
A.D. 300 – 800	Rocketry at low ebb of activity owing to Dark Ages, Goths, Vandalism, Vizigoths, Ostragoths and other forms of Ostracism.
1066	King Harold Godwinson receives fatal direct hit by guided missile built in Normandy.
1130	First rocket missiles (Chinese) used for civilising and entertaining.
1452	Wars of the Roses. York bombed by Lancasters.
1550	Tudors developed.
1605	Gunpowder Plot (early attempt to propel His Majesty's Government into Outer Space) Failure attributable to poor Security.
1684	Newton's law of gravity passed (space flight at last possible).
1718	South Sea Bubble (supported by hot air).
1725	Flight of the Walloons (from the Netherlands).
1783	Flight of Balloons (from Versailles – Montgolfier).
1865	Jules Verne's alleged flight to the Moon (now considered doubtful).
1898	Ohm's Law passed by both Houses.
1903	Powered flight proved to be impossible (Newcomb).
1903	First powered flight (Wright).
1921–2	Rapid developments in Ireland. The Four Courts, The Post Office, and other parts of Dublin successfully put into free orbit by the Irish Rocketry Association.
1933	Formation of British Interplanetary Society (all experiments categorically forbidden by the Home Office).

1934	Revision of the Mental Deficiency Acts.
1935	*Jet Propulsion in the Third Reich* (A. Schickelgruberfarben).
1936	Jet propulsion shown to be completely impractical (Foreign Office).
1938	Doppelganger's Discrepancy.
1940–44	*Kreigrackettenhauptausfarhtsellschaft* (Werner von Braun, U.S.A.)
1950	The Great Controversy starts.
	Schrimpwisl expelled from the R.A.S.
1952	Schrimpwisl's First Attempt.
1954	Schrimpwisl's Second Attempt.
1955	Schrimpwisl pronounced out of danger.
1956	Schrimpwisl's Third Attempt (protest meeting by the Flat Earth Society at Caxton Hall).
1957	First Russian Sputnik, shortly to be followed by First American Sputnik, shortly to be followed by Second Russian Sputnik, shortly to be followed by 290 other miscellaneous and assorted sputniks.
1959	Schrimpwisl's Fourth Attempt.
1963	Schrimpwisl's Fifth Attempt.
1968	Intermediate and Pointless Attempt in association with Uprichard.
1968 (June)	Schrimpwisl's Seventh Attempt.
1969	Landing of the British Orbital Space Station on the Moon under the Captaincy of Sir Humphrey ffryde-Fischer, Bt., O.M., etc.
1969	Boyle's Law finally repealed through diligent perseverence of Sir Humphrey ffryde-Fischer, Bt., O.M., etc.
1969	Americans also go to the Moon.
1971 (September)	Schrimpwisl's Final Attempt.
1972	Sir Humphrey ffryde-Fischer honoured for his achievements with an Illuminated Address presented in absentio by the Moreton Hampstead Third Troup Sea Scouts. Several lines of favourable mention in the *South Devon Examiner* and the *Barnstaple Weekly Advertiser*.